play & learn
activity cubes

Have a play day with your baby as you go fishing, follow a colorful rainbow, or smell beautiful flowers. Every side will be a great adventure and give hours of learning fun. Each cube has texture, mirrors, or sliders to keep your little one busy.

LEISURE ARTS, INC. • Maumelle, Arkansas

table of
contents

basic square

Finished Size: 6½" (16.5 cm) square

Rnd 1 (Right side)**:** With color indicated in individual instructions and using an adjustable loop to form a ring *(Figs. 1a-d, page 45)*, work 8 sc in ring; do **not** join, place marker to indicate beginning of rnd *(see Markers, page 44)*.

Note: Loop a short piece of yarn around any stitch to mark Rnd 1 as **right** side.

Rnd 2: (Ch 2, sc in next 2 sc) 4 times: 8 sc and 4 corner ch-2 sps.

Rnd 3: ★ (Sc, ch 2, sc) in next corner ch-2 sp, sc in next 2 sc; repeat from ★ around: 16 sc and 4 corner ch-2 sps.

Rnds 4-15: ★ Sc in each sc across to next corner ch-2 sp, (sc, ch 2, sc) in corner ch-2 sp; repeat from ★ around, sc in each sc across: 112 sc and 4 corner ch-2 sps.

Slip st in next sc; finish off.

JOINING

With **wrong** sides together and using Diagram on page 5 as a guide for placement, join 4 Squares to center Square as follows:

With color indicated in individual instructions and working through **both** loops of sc on **both** pieces, join yarn with sc in any corner ch-2 sp *(see Joining With Sc, page 44)*; sc in each sc across to next corner ch-2 sp, sc in corner ch-2 sp, ★ working through **both** loops of sc on **next** Square and center Square, sc in same corner ch-2 sp as last sc on center Square and in any corner ch-2 sp on **next** Square, sc in each sc across to next corner ch-2 sp, sc in corner ch-2 sp; repeat from ★ 2 times **more**, ending by working last sc in same corner ch-2 sp on center Square as first sc; join with slip st to first sc, finish off.

Using remaining Square as center, repeat Joining around opposite sides of Squares.

SIDE SEAM

With **wrong** sides together and working through **both** loops of sts across any unjoined edge, join color indicated in individual instructions with sc in any corner ch-2 sp; sc in each sc across to next corner ch-2 sp, sc in corner ch-2 sp; finish off.

Repeat Side Seam across each unjoined edge, stuffing Block with polyester fiberfill before closing.

Thread upholstery needle with a long strand of Square color yarn. Sew through middle of one Square and come out through middle of Square on opposite side of Block twice. Secure ends.

Repeat with remaining Squares of Block.

DIAGRAM

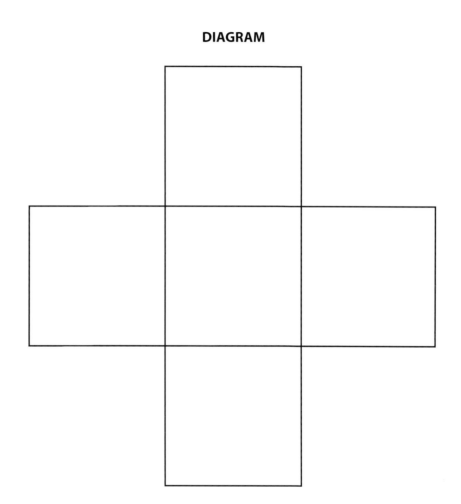

flower power cube

Finished Size:

Approximately 6½" (16.5 cm) cube

 **EASY**

SHOPPING LIST

Yarn (Medium Weight) 🄸4

[7 ounces, 364 yards
(198 grams, 333 meters) per skein]:

☐ Lt Green - 75 yards
   (68.5 meters)

☐ Green - 75 yards (68.5 meters)

☐ Dk Green - 60 yards (55 meters)

☐ Navy - 60 yards (55 meters)

☐ Dk Aqua - 60 yards (55 meters)

☐ Purple - 60 yards (55 meters)

☐ Black - 30 yards (27.5 meters)

☐ Yellow - 30 yards (27.5 meters)

☐ White - 25 yards (23 meters)

☐ Variegated - 20 yards
   (18.5 meters)

☐ Orange - 5 yards (4.5 meters)

☐ Gold - 5 yards (4.5 meters)

☐ Lt Purple - small amount

☐ Red - small amount

Crochet Hook

☐ Size H (5 mm)
   or size needed for gauge

Additional Supplies

☐ Yarn needle

☐ Upholstery needle

☐ Polyester fiberfill

☐ Hole punch

☐ Flexible mirror sheet

☐ Rattle

☐ Linking teething rings - 6 links

STITCH GUIDE -----

TREBLE CROCHET *(abbreviated tr)*

YO twice, insert hook in st indicated, YO and pull up a loop (4 loops on hook), (YO and draw through 2 loops on hook) 3 times.

SINGLE CROCHET 2 TOGETHER *(abbreviated sc2tog)*

Pull up a loop in each of next 2 sc, YO and draw through all 3 loops on hook **(counts as one sc)**.

- - - - - - - - - - - - - - - - - - -

BLOCK

Make 6 Squares: One **each** with Green (Top), Dk Aqua (Side 1), Navy (Side 2), Lt Green (Side 3), Purple (Side 4), and Dk Green (bottom) **(see Basic Square, page 4)**.

With Black, work Joinings and Side Seams.

When **right** side is indicated, loop a short piece of yarn around any stitch on same row or round **(now and throughout)**.

Use photos as guides for placement of all pieces. For embroidery, refer to Figs. 4-7, page 46.

TOP
FLOWER
CENTER

Rnd 1 (Right side)**:** With Yellow and using an adjustable loop to form a ring, work 6 sc in ring; place marker to indicate beginning of rnd.

Rnd 2: 2 Sc in each sc around: 12 sc.

Rnd 3: (Sc in next sc, 2 sc in next sc) around: 18 sc.

Rnd 4: (Sc in next 2 sc, 2 sc in next sc) around changing to Gold in last sc **(Fig. A)**: 24 sc.

Fig. A

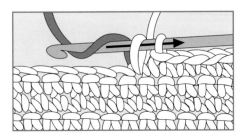

Rnd 5: (Sc in next 3 sc, 2 sc in next sc) around: 30 sc.

Rnds 6 and 7: Sc in each sc around.

Slip st in next sc; finish off leaving a long end.

With Black and using straight st, add eyes and mouth.

PETAL (Make 10)
With White, ch 7.

Row 1 (Right side)**:** Dc in third ch from hook and in next 3 chs, 5 dc in last ch; working in free loops of beginning ch **(Fig. 2b, page 45)**, dc in next 3 chs, 3 dc in next ch; join with slip st to first st, finish off leaving a long end.

Sew end of each Petal to Back Loops Only of 3 sc on Center **(Fig. 3, page 45)**.

STEM
With Lt Green, ch 10.

Row 1 (Right side)**:** Hdc in third ch from hook and in each ch across; finish off leaving a long end.

Sew Stem to Green Square; then sew Flower Center to Square at top of Stem.

SIDE 1

STEM

With Lt Green, ch 30.

Row 1 (Right side)**:** Hdc in third ch from hook and in each ch across; finish off leaving a long end.

Sew Stem to Dk Aqua Square.

TOP LEAF

Rnd 1 (Right side)**:** With Green, ch 3, 11 dc in third ch from hook; join with slip st to top of beginning ch: 12 sts.

Rnd 2: Sc in next dc, (dc, tr, ch 2, tr, dc) in next dc, 2 sc in each of next 6 dc, leave remaining sts unworked; finish off leaving a long end.

BOTTOM LEAF

Rnd 1 (Right side)**:** With Green, ch 3, 11 dc in third ch from hook; join with slip st to top of beginning ch: 12 sts.

Rnd 2: 2 Sc in each of next 6 dc, (dc, tr, ch 2, tr, dc) in next dc, sc in next dc, slip st in next dc, leave remaining sts unworked; finish off leaving a long end.

Sew bottom edge and ends of Leaves to Square.

FINGER PUPPETS

LADYBUG (Make 2)

Body (Right side)**:** With Red, ch 3, 11 dc in third ch from hook; join with slip st to top of beginning ch, finish off: 12 sts.

Head: With **right** side facing, join Black with slip st in same st as joining; skip next dc, 4 dc in next dc, skip next dc, slip st in next dc, leave remaining dc unworked; finish off.

With Black and using straight st, add dots and stripe on one Body. With White and using satin st, add eyes to Head on same piece.

With **wrong** sides together and matching sts, sew pieces together leaving bottom 4 dc of Body free.

Join Black with slip st at bottom of back Body; ch 50 **tightly**; slip st around sc on Square behind Top Leaf; finish off.

BUMBLE BEE (Make 2)

Body (Right side)**:** With Yellow, ch 3, 11 dc in third ch from hook; join with slip st to top of beginning ch, finish off: 12 sts.

Head: With **right** side facing, join Black with slip st in same st as joining; skip next dc, 4 dc in next dc, skip next dc, slip st in next dc, leave remaining dc unworked; finish off.

Wings: With White, (ch 2, 6 sc in second ch from hook) twice; finish off leaving a long end.

With **wrong** sides together and matching sts, sew pieces together leaving bottom 4 dc of Body free.

With Black and using straight st, add stripes around Body.

Sew center of Wings to Body.

Antennae: Join Black with slip st at back of Head, ch 3 **tightly**; finish off leaving a ¼" (6 mm) end.

Repeat for second Antennae.

Join Black with slip st at bottom of back Body; ch 50 **tightly**; slip st around sc on Square behind Bottom Leaf; finish off.

SIDE 2
FLOWERS

CENTER (Make 6)

Rnd 1 (Right side): With Yellow and using an adjustable loop to form a ring, work 12 dc in ring; join with slip st to first dc, finish off.

FRONT PETALS

(Make one **each** with Orange, Dk Aqua, and Purple)

Rnd 1: With **right** side of one Center facing, join color indicated with sc in any dc; 3 sc in Front Loop Only of next dc (*Fig. 3, page 45*), (sc in **both** loops of next dc, 3 sc in Front Loop Only of next dc) around; join with slip st to first sc, finish off: 24 sc.

With **wrong** sides of front and back Centers together, sew 2 sc together; skip next 4 sc on each piece, then sew next 2 sc together.

SLIDE (Make 3)

With Lt Green and leaving a long end, ch 24; finish off leaving a long end.

Insert each Slide through a Flower.

Sew Slides to Navy Square.

GRASS

Row 1 (Right side): With Lt Green, work 21 fdc (*see Foundation Double Crochet, page 44*).

Rows 2 and 3: Ch 3 (**counts as first dc, now and throughout**), turn; dc in next st and in each st across.

Finish off leaving a long end.

With **right** side facing, sew 3 sides of Grass to bottom edge of Square, leaving top edge free.

SIDE 2

SIDE 3
POCKET

With Lt Green, ch 10.

Row 1: Dc in third ch from hook and in next 6 chs, 6 dc in last ch; working in free loops of beginning ch, dc in next 7 chs; do **not** join: 21 sts.

Row 2 (Right side)**:** Ch 3, turn; dc in next 6 dc, 2 dc in each of next 6 dc, dc in last 8 sts: 27 dc.

Row 3: Ch 3, turn; dc in next 7 dc, 2 dc in next dc, (dc in next dc, 2 dc in next dc) 5 times, dc in last 8 dc: 33 dc.

Row 4: Ch 3, turn; dc in next 8 dc, 2 dc in next dc, (dc in next 2 dc, 2 dc in next dc) 5 times, dc in last 8 dc: 39 dc.

Edging: Ch 1, do **not** turn; work 16 sc evenly spaced across ends of rows; finish off leaving a long end.

With **right** side facing, sew Pocket to Lt Green Square.

FLOWER RATTLE
FLOWER CENTER

Rnd 1 (Right side)**:** With Yellow and using an adjustable loop to form a ring, work 6 sc in ring; place marker to indicate beginning of rnd.

Rnd 2: 2 Sc in each sc around: 12 sc.

Rnd 3: (Sc in next sc, 2 sc in next sc) around: 18 sc.

Rnd 4: (Sc in next 2 sc, 2 sc in next sc) around: 24 sc.

Rnd 5: Sc in each sc around changing to Variegated in last sc; cut Yellow.

Rnds 6 and 7: Working in Back Loops Only, sc in each sc around.

Rnd 8: Working in both loops, (sc2tog, sc in next 2 sc) around: 18 sc.

Stuff Center with polyester fiberfill, placing rattle in center.

Rnd 9: (Sc2tog, sc in next sc) around: 12 sc.

Rnd 10: Sc2tog around: 6 sc.

Continue to sc2tog until hole is closed; finish off.

PETALS

Rnd 1: With **right** side facing and working in free loops of Rnd 5 *(Fig. 2a, page 45)*, join Variegated with sc in first sc; skip next sc, 5 dc in next sc, skip next sc, ★ sc in next sc, skip next sc, 5 dc in next sc, skip next sc; repeat from ★ 4 times **more**: 6 petals.

Rnd 2: Working in free loops of Rnd 6, (slip st, sc) in next sc, ★ skip next sc, 5 dc in next sc, skip next sc, sc in next sc; repeat from ★ 4 times **more**, 5 dc in next sc, skip next slip st, slip st in next sc; finish off: 6 petals.

HANDLE

Rnd 1 (Right side): With Green and using an adjustable loop to form a ring, work 6 sc in ring; do **not** join, place marker to indicate beginning of rnd.

Rnd 2: 2 Sc in each sc around: 12 sc.

Rnd 3: (Sc in next 2 sc, 2 sc in next sc) around: 16 sc.

Rnd 4: Sc in Back Loop Only of each sc around.

Stuff Handle with polyester fiberfill as you crochet.

Rnds 5-20: Sc in both loops of each sc around.

Slip st in next sc; finish off leaving a long end.

Sew Handle to back of Flower.

LEAF (Make 2)
With Green, ch 7.

Rnd 1 (Right side): Slip st in second ch from hook, sc in next ch, hdc in next ch, dc in next ch, hdc in next ch, 3 sc in last ch; working in free loops of beginning ch, hdc in next ch, dc in next ch, hdc in next ch, sc in next ch, slip st in next ch; finish off leaving a long end.

Sew Leaves to Handle.

SIDE 4
FLOWER POT

With Orange, ch 5.

Row 1: Sc in second ch from hook and in each ch across: 4 sc.

Rows 2-4: Ch 1, turn; sc in each sc across.

Edging: Ch 1, turn; (sc, ch 1, sc) in first sc, sc evenly around working (sc, ch 1, sc) in each corner; join with slip st to first sc, finish off leaving a long end.

RIM

With Orange, ch 9.

Row 1: Sc in second ch from hook and in each ch across; finish off leaving a long end.

Sew Rim to top edge of Flower Pot; then sew Flower Pot to Purple Square, leaving top edge free.

STEM

With Green, ch 12.

Row 1 (Wrong side): Sc in second ch from hook and in each ch across; finish off leaving a long end.

LEAF (Make 2)

With Green, ch 8.

Rnd 1 (Right side): Slip st in second ch from hook, sc in next ch, hdc in next ch, dc in next 2 chs, hdc in next ch, 3 sc in last ch; working in free loops of beginning ch, hdc in next ch, dc in next 2 chs, hdc in next ch, sc in next ch, slip st in next ch; finish off leaving a long end.

Sew Stem to Square.
Sew ends of Leaves to Stem; then sew tips of Leaves in place around teething rings.

SIDE 4

FLOWER

With Lt Purple, ch 6; join with slip st to form a ring.

Rnd 1 (Right side)**:** (Slip st, 2 dc, slip st) in next 5 chs; finish off leaving a long end.

With Yellow, add 5 straight sts for center.

Sew center of Flower to Square.

BOTTOM
FRAME

With Variegated, ch 30; being careful **not** to twist ch, join with slip st to form a ring.

Rnd 1 (Right side)**:** Ch 3, dc in next 3 chs, 2 dc in next ch, (dc in next 4 chs, 2 dc in next ch) around; join with slip st to first dc: 36 dc.

Rnd 2: Ch 1, sc in same st as joining and in next 7 dc, 2 sc in next dc, (sc in next 8 dc, 2 sc in next dc) around; join with slip st to first sc: 40 sc.

Rnd 3: Ch 1, sc in same st as joining, skip next sc, 5 dc in next sc, skip next sc, ★ sc in next sc, skip next sc, 5 dc in next sc, skip next sc; repeat from ★ around; join with slip st to first sc, finish off leaving a long end.

MIRROR

Using pattern below, cut a 2¾" (7 cm) diameter circle from reflective sheet, making sure it will fit under Frame. Punch 4 evenly spaced holes around edge of circle.

Sew mirror to center of Dk Green Square; then with **right** side facing, sew Frame in place.

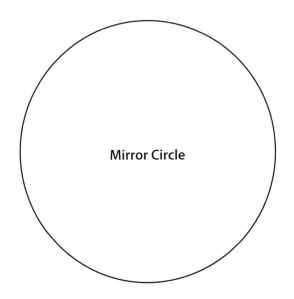

Mirror Circle

BOTTOM

fish
cube

Finished Size:

Approximately 6½" (16.5 cm) cube

EASY

SHOPPING LIST

Yarn (Medium Weight) 4

[7 ounces, 364 yards
(198 grams, 333 meters) per skein]:

- ☐ Tan - 140 yards (128 meters)
- ☐ Dk Aqua - 130 yards (119 meters)
- ☐ Lt Blue - 120 yards (110 meters)
- ☐ Navy - 50 yards (46 meters)
- ☐ Blue - 30 yards (27.5 meters)
- ☐ Lt Green - 15 yards (13.5 meters)
- ☐ Red - 15 yards (13.5 meters)
- ☐ Yellow - 10 yards (9 meters)
- ☐ Black - 10 yards (9 meters)
- ☐ Lt Purple - 10 yards (9 meters)
- ☐ Dk Grey - 5 yards (4.5 meters)
- ☐ Orange - 5 yards (4.5 meters)
- ☐ Purple - small amount
- ☐ Pink - small amount
- ☐ Lt Pink - small amount
- ☐ Gold - small amount
- ☐ Burgundy - small amount

Crochet Hook

- ☐ Size H (5 mm)

or size needed for gauge

Additional Supplies

- ☐ Yarn needle
- ☐ Upholstery needle
- ☐ Polyester fiberfill
- ☐ Hole punch
- ☐ Flexible mirror sheet
- ☐ Crinkle material plastic film
- ☐ 1" (2.5 cm) plastic ring - 3

STITCH GUIDE - - - - -

TREBLE CROCHET *(abbreviated tr)*

YO twice, insert hook in dc indicated, YO and pull up a loop (4 loops on hook), (YO and draw through 2 loops on hook) 3 times.

SINGLE CROCHET 2 TOGETHER *(abbreviated sc2tog)*

Pull up a loop in each of next 2 sc, YO and draw through all 3 loops on hook **(counts as one sc)**.

SINGLE CROCHET 3 TOGETHER *(abbreviated sc3tog)*

Pull up a loop in each of next 3 sc, YO and draw through all 4 loops on hook **(counts as one sc)**.

- - - - - - - - - - - - - - - - -

BLOCK

Make 6 Squares - 2 **each** with Lt Blue, Dk Aqua, and Tan *(see Basic Square, page 4)*.

With Navy and having same color Squares opposite each other, work Joining and Side Seams.

When **right** side is indicated, loop a short piece of yarn around any stitch on same row or round **(now and throughout)**.

Use photos as guides for placement of all pieces. For embroidery, refer to Figs. 4-7, page 46.

TOP
LARGE MIRROR FRAME

With Blue, ch 30; being careful **not** to twist ch, join with slip st to form a ring.

Rnd 1 (Right side)**:** Ch 3 **(counts as first dc, now and throughout)**, dc in next 4 chs, 2 dc in next ch, (dc in next 5 chs, 2 dc in next ch) around; join with slip st to first dc, finish off leaving a long end.

MEDIUM MIRROR FRAME

With Blue, ch 25; being careful **not** to twist ch, join with slip st to form a ring.

Rnd 1 (Right side)**:** Ch 3, dc in next 3 chs, 2 dc in next ch, (dc in next 4 chs, 2 dc in next ch) around; join with slip st to first dc, finish off leaving a long end.

SMALL MIRROR FRAME

With Blue, ch 20; being careful **not** to twist ch, join with slip st to form a ring.

Rnd 1 (Right side)**:** Ch 3, dc in next 2 chs, 2 dc in next ch, (dc in next 3 chs, 2 dc in next ch) around; join with slip st to first dc, finish off leaving a long end.

MIRRORS

Using patterns on page 21, cut 2" (5 cm), 2½" (6.5 cm) and 2¾" (7 cm) diameter circles from reflective sheet, making sure each will fit under its Frame. Punch 4 evenly spaced holes around edge of each circle. Sew mirrors to one Lt Blue Square.

LARGE BUBBLE

With Blue and using an adjustable loop to form a ring, work 12 dc in ring; join with slip st to first dc, finish off leaving a long end.

SMALL BUBBLE (Make 2)

With Blue and using an adjustable loop to form a ring, work 6 dc in ring; join with slip st to first dc, finish off leaving a long end.

Sew Bubbles and Mirror Frames to Square.

Small Mirror Circle

Medium Mirror Circle

Large Mirror Circle

TOP

SIDE 1

SIDE 1
POCKET (Make 3)
With Tan, ch 11.

Row 1: Dc in third ch from hook and in next 7 chs, 6 dc in last ch; working in free loops of beginning ch *(Fig. 2b, page 45)*, dc in next 8 chs: 22 dc.

Row 2 (Right side)**:** Ch 3, turn; dc in next 7 dc, 2 dc in each of next 6 dc, dc in next 8 dc, ch 1; work 8 sc evenly spaced across ends of rows; finish off leaving a long end.

Work one Trim **each** with Red, Yellow, and Blue.

Trim: With **right** side facing, join color indicated with hdc in first sc *(see Joining with Hdc, page 44)*; hdc in each sc across; finish off.

Sew Pockets to one Tan Square.

FISH (Make one **each** with Red, Yellow, and Blue)

Rnd 1 (Right side)**:** With color indicated, ch 2, 6 sc in second ch from hook; do **not** join, place marker to indicate beginning of rnd.

Rnd 2: Sc in each sc around.

Rnd 3: (Sc in next 2 sc, 3 sc in next sc) twice: 10 sc.

Rnds 4-6: Sc in each sc around.

Rnd 7: (Sc in next 4 sc, 3 sc in next sc) twice: 14 sc.

Rnd 8: Sc in each sc around.

Stuff Fish with polyester fiberfill.

Rnd 9: (Sc in next 4 sc, sc3tog) twice: 10 sc.

Rnd 10: Sc in each sc around.

Rnd 11: (Sc in next 2 sc, sc3tog) twice: 6 sc.

Slip st in next sc; finish off leaving a long end.

With Black and using straight st, add eyes.

TOP FIN (Make one **each** with Burgundy, Gold, and Navy)

Row 1: With color indicated, ch 4, (slip st, sc) in second ch from hook, 2 sc in next ch, (sc, slip st) in last ch; finish off leaving a long end.

TAIL FIN (Make one **each** with Burgundy, Gold, and Navy)

Rnd 1: With color indicated and leaving a long end, ch 3, 4 dc in third ch from hook (**2 skipped chs count as first dc**), ch 1, sc around last dc; working in free loop of beginning ch, 3 sc in ch, sc around first dc, ch 2, 2 sc in each of next 5 dc, ch 2; join with slip st to first sc, finish off.

Sew Fins to Fish.
With same color as Fins and using straight st, add side Fins.

Sew plastic ring to Fish.

SIDE 2

BODY (Make 2 **each** with Orange, Lt Green, and Lt Purple)

Rnd 1 (Right side)**:** With color indicated and using an adjustable loop to form a ring, work 12 dc in ring, slip st in first dc, ch 3, 4 dc in same st (tail); finish off leaving a long end on one Body only.

With Black and using straight st, add eyes to each Body. Add the number 1 to each Orange Body, the number 2 to each Lt Green Body, and the number 3 to each Lt Purple Body.

With **wrong** sides of Bodies together, sew tail together. Using matching color, sew 3 dc together opposite the tail.

SLIDE (Make 3)

With Dk Aqua and leaving a long end, work 24 fsc *(see Foundation Single Crochet, page 44)*; finish off leaving a long end.

Insert each Slide through center of one Fish.

Sew Slides to one Dk Aqua Square in numerical order.

SIDE 3
POCKET
With Tan, ch 10.

Row 1: Dc in fourth ch from hook (**3 skipped chs count as first dc**) and in next 5 chs, 6 dc in last ch; working in free loops of beginning ch, dc in next 7 chs: 20 dc.

Row 2 (Right side): Ch 3, turn; dc in next 6 dc, 2 dc in each of next 6 dc, dc in last 7 dc: 26 dc.

Row 3: Ch 3, turn; dc in next 7 dc, 2 dc in next dc, (dc in next dc, 2 dc in next dc) 5 times, dc in last 7 dc: 32 dc.

Row 4: Ch 3, turn; dc in next 6 dc, 2 dc in next dc, (dc in next 2 dc, 2 dc in next dc) 5 times, dc in last 9 dc: 38 dc.

Trim: Ch 1, do **not** turn; work 16 sc evenly spaced across ends of rows; finish off leaving a long end.

Sew Pocket to corner of remaining Tan Square.

FISHING ROD
HANDLE
Rnd 1: With Red, ch 2, 6 sc in second ch from hook; do **not** join, place marker to indicate beginning of rnd.

Rnd 2: 2 Sc in each sc around: 12 sc.

Rnd 3: (Sc in next 2 sc, 2 sc in next sc) around: 16 sc.

Rnd 4: Sc in Back Loop Only of each sc around *(Fig. 3, page 45)*.

Rnds 5-17: Sc in both loops of each sc around.

Rnd 18: Working in Back Loops Only, (sc2tog, sc in next 2 sc) around: 12 sc.

Stuff Handle firmly with polyester fiberfill.

Rnd 19: Working in both loops, (sc2tog, sc in next sc) around: 8 sc.

Rnd 20: Sc2tog around: 4 sc.

Continue to sc2tog until hole is closed; finish off.

HOOK
SHANK
Rnd 1 (Right side)**:** With Dk Grey, ch 2, 6 sc in second ch from hook.

Rnds 2-5: Sc in each sc around.

Do **not** finish off, stuff Shank firmly with polyester fiberfill.

Closing: Flatten top of Shank, working through **both** loops of **both** layers, sc in next 2 sc; finish off.

CURVE
Work same as Shank through Rnd 4.

Slip st in next sc; finish off leaving a long end.

Stuff Curve firmly with polyester fiberfill.

TIP
Work same as Shank through Rnd 3.

Slip st in next sc; finish off leaving a long end.

Stuff Tip firmly with polyester fiberfill.

Sew Curve at an angle to beginning end of Shank; then sew Tip at an angle to beginning end of Curve.

FISHING LINE AND ROD

Join Black with sc to end of Shank; ch 22.

Rnd 1 (Right side)**:** 6 Sc in second ch from hook, do **not** join, place marker to indicate beginning of rnd.

Rnd 2: Sc in each sc around.

Rnd 3: Working in Back Loops Only, (sc in next 2 sc, 2 sc in next sc) twice: 8 sc.

Rnds 4-16: Working in both loops, sc in each sc around.

Stuff Rod firmly with polyester fiberfill.

Slip st in next sc; finish off leaving a long end.

Sew Rod to Handle.

SIDE 4
JELLYFISH
BODY

With Lt Purple, ch 7.

Row 1 (Right side)**:** Dc in third ch from hook and in next 3 chs, 6 dc in last ch; working in free loops of beginning ch, dc in next 4 chs: 14 dc.

Row 2: Ch 3, turn; dc in next 3 dc, 2 dc in each of next 6 dc, dc in last 4 dc: 20 dc.

Edging Rnd: Ch 3, turn; 5 dc in first dc, dc in next 6 dc, 2 dc in each of next 6 dc, dc in next 6 dc, 6 dc in last dc; working in ends of rows, sc in end of Row 1, 6 dc in next ch, sc in end of Row 1; join with slip st to first dc, finish off leaving a long end.

With Purple and using straight st, add eyes and mouth to Body.

TENTACLES
PINK (Make 2)

With Pink, (ch 3, sc in second ch from hook) 9 times, ch 2; finish off leaving a long end.

LT PINK (Make 2)

With Lt Pink, (ch 3, dc in third ch from hook) 5 times, finish off leaving a long end.

PURPLE (Make 3)

With Purple, ch 20 **tightly**; finish off leaving a long end.

SEAWEED
LARGE SEAWEED

With Lt Green and leaving a long end, ch 40.

Row 1: 3 Sc in second ch from hook and in each ch across; finish off leaving a long end.

SMALL SEAWEED

With Lt Green and leaving a long end, ch 15.

Row 1: 3 Sc in second ch from hook and in each ch across; finish off leaving a long end.

Sew Tentacles to **wrong** side of Body; knot remaining end and trim.
Sew Jellyfish to remaining Dk Aqua Square, stuffing with crinkle material before closing.
Sew top and bottom of Seaweed to Square.

BOTTOM
BOTTOM WAVE

Row 1: With Navy, work 21 fdc *(see Foundation Double Crochet, page 44)*.

Rows 2-5: Ch 3, turn; dc in next st and in each st across.

Row 6 (Right side)**:** Turn; slip st in first dc, sc in next dc, hdc in next dc, dc in next dc, (tr, ch 2, tr) in next dc, ★ dc in next dc, hdc in next dc, sc in next dc, slip st in next dc, sc in next dc, hdc in next dc, dc in next dc, (tr, ch 2, tr) in next dc; repeat from ★ once **more**; finish off leaving a long end.

TOP WAVE

Rows 1-4: With Blue, work same as Bottom Wave: 21 dc.

Row 5 (Right side)**:** Ch 4, turn; dc in next dc, hdc in next dc, sc in next dc, ★ slip st in next dc, sc in next dc, hdc in next dc, dc in next dc, (tr, ch 2, tr) in next dc, dc in next dc, hdc in next dc, sc in next dc; repeat from ★ once **more**, slip st in last dc; finish off leaving a long end.

Sew sides and bottom edge of Bottom Wave to remaining Lt Blue Square leaving sts on Row 6 free; then sew Top Wave under edge of Bottom Wave in same manner.

rainbow cube

Finished Size:

Approximately 6½" (16.5 cm) cube

■■□□ **EASY**

SHOPPING LIST

Yarn (Medium Weight) 4

[7 ounces, 364 yards
(198 grams, 333 meters) per skein]:

- ☐ White - 1 skein
- ☐ Variegated - 50 yards
  (46 meters)
- ☐ Blue - 30 yards (27.5 meters)
- ☐ Yellow - 25 yards (23 meters)
- ☐ Dk Green - 20 yards
  (18.5 meters)
- ☐ Orange - 15 yards (13.5 meters)
- ☐ Red - 10 yards (9 meters)
- ☐ Grey - 5 yards (4.5 meters)
- ☐ Black - small amount

Crochet Hook

- ☐ Size H (5 mm)
  or size needed for gauge

Additional Supplies

- ☐ Yarn needle
- ☐ Upholstery needle
- ☐ Polyester fiberfill
- ☐ 1⅛" (28 mm) button - one **each**
  Red, Orange, Yellow, Green,
  and Blue
- ☐ Hole punch
- ☐ Flexible mirror sheet
- ☐ Crinkle material plastic film
- ☐ Linking teething rings - 6 links

STITCH GUIDE - - - - -

TREBLE CROCHET *(abbreviated tr)*

YO twice, insert hook in dc indicated, YO and pull up a loop (4 loops on hook), (YO and draw through 2 loops on hook) 3 times.

- -

BLOCK

With White, make 6 Squares *(see Basic Square, page 4)*.

With Variegated, work Joining and Side Seams.

When **right** side is indicated, loop a short piece of yarn around any stitch on same row or round (**now and throughout**).

Use photos as guides for placement of all pieces. For embroidery, refer to Figs. 4-7, page 46.

TOP
MIRROR FRAME

With Variegated, ch 60; being careful **not** to twist ch, join with slip st to form a ring.

Rnd 1 (Right side)**:** Ch 3 (**counts as first dc, now and throughout**), dc in next 8 chs, 2 dc in next ch, (dc in next 9 chs, 2 dc in next ch) around; join with slip st to first dc, finish off leaving a long end.

MIRROR

Using pattern below, cut a 4¼" (11 cm) diameter circle from reflective sheet, making sure it will fit under Frame. Punch 4 evenly spaced holes around edge of circle.

Sew mirror to center of one Square; then with **right** side facing, sew Frame in place.

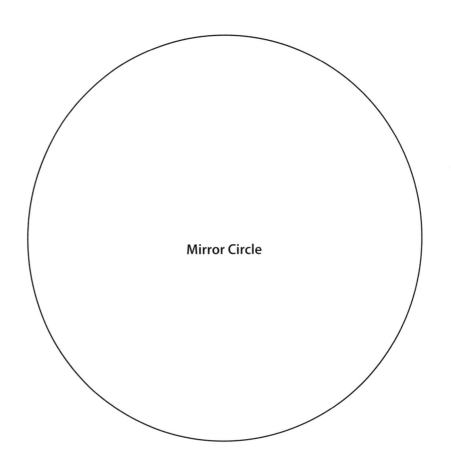

Mirror Circle

SIDE 1
RAINBOW
FIRST ARCH

Row 1: With Blue, ch 3, 6 dc in third ch from hook.

Row 2: Ch 3, turn; dc in same st, 2 dc in next dc and in each dc across: 12 dc.

Row 3: Ch 3, turn; 2 dc in next dc, (dc in next dc, 2 dc in next dc) across: 18 dc.

Row 4: Ch 3, turn; dc in next dc, 2 dc in next dc, (dc in next 2 dc, 2 dc in next dc) across: 24 dc.

Row 5: Ch 3, turn; dc in next 2 dc, 2 dc in next dc, (dc in next 3 dc, 2 dc in next dc) across: 30 dc.

Row 6: Ch 3, turn; dc in next 3 dc, 2 dc in next dc, (dc in next 4 dc, 2 dc in next dc) across: 36 dc.

Trim (Right side)**:** Ch 2, do **not** turn; work 23 sc evenly spaced across ends of rows; finish off leaving a long end.

SECOND ARCH

Rows 1-5: With Green, work same as First Arch: 30 dc.

Trim (Right side)**:** Ch 2, do **not** turn; work 19 sc evenly spaced across ends of rows; finish off leaving a long end.

THIRD ARCH

Rows 1-4: With Yellow, work same as First Arch: 24 dc.

Trim (Right side)**:** Ch 2, do **not** turn; work 17 sc evenly spaced across ends of rows; finish off leaving a long end.

FOURTH ARCH

Rows 1-3: With Orange, work same as First Arch: 18 dc.

Trim (Right side)**:** Ch 2, do **not** turn; work 13 sc evenly spaced across ends of rows; finish off leaving a long end.

FIFTH ARCH

Rows 1 and 2: With Red, work same as First Arch: 12 dc.

Trim (Right side)**:** Ch 2, do **not** turn; work 9 sc evenly spaced across ends of rows; finish off leaving a long end.

SUN

Rnd 1 (Right side)**:** With Yellow, ch 2, 6 sc in second ch from hook; do **not** join, place marker to indicate beginning of rnd.

Rnd 2: 2 Sc in each sc around: 12 sc.

Rnd 3: (Sc in next sc, 2 sc in next sc) around: 18 sc.

Rnd 4: (Sc in next 2 sc, 2 sc in next sc) around: 24 sc.

Slip st in next sc; finish off leaving a long end.

With Black and using straight st, add eyes and mouth to Sun.

Sew Sun to center of one Side Square. With Yellow and using straight st, add rays.

Sew bottom edge of Rainbow Arches to same Square.

SIDE 2
LOOP (Make 1 **each** with Red, Yellow, and Blue)

Row 1: With color indicated, work 10 fsc (*see Foundation Single Crochet, page 44*).

Rows 2 and 3: Ch 1, turn; sc in each st across.

Finish off leaving a long end.

Fold piece in half and sew short edges together.

With White and using straight st, embroider the number 1 on Red Loop, the number 2 on Yellow Loop, and the number 3 on Blue Loop.

Sew Loops to one Side Square in numerical order; then attach corresponding number of teething rings to Loops.

SIDE 3
CLOUD
With Grey, ch 21.

Rnd 1 (Right side)**:** Dc in third ch from hook and in next 17 chs, 6 dc in next ch; working in free loops of beginning ch (*Fig. 2b, page 45*), dc in next 17 chs, 4 dc in next ch; do **not** join, place marker to indicate beginning of rnd: 45 dc.

Rnd 2: Slip st in next dc, sc in next dc, hdc in next dc, skip next 2 dc, 4 tr in next dc, dc in next 7 dc, 4 tr in next dc, skip next 2 dc, hdc in next dc, sc in next dc, slip st in next dc, leave remaining sts unworked.

Rnd 3 (Right side)**: Turn**; slip st in first 7 sts, hdc in next dc, skip next 2 dc, 6 tr in next dc, skip next 2 dc, hdc in next dc, slip st in next 13 sts, sc in next dc, skip next 2 dc, 6 tr in next dc, skip next 2 dc, dc in next dc, skip next 2 dc, 6 tr in next dc, skip next 2 dc, sc in next dc, slip st in next 7 sts; join with slip st to first slip st, finish off leaving a long end.

With Black and using straight st, add eyes and mouth to Cloud.

RAINDROP
BODY (Make 2 **each** with Red, Orange, Yellow, Dk Green, and Blue)

With color indicated, ch 5.

Rnd 1 (Right side)**:** Slip st in second ch from hook, sc in next ch, hdc in next ch, 6 dc in next ch; working in free loops of beginning ch, hdc in next ch, sc in next ch, slip st in next ch; finish off leaving a long end on one Body of each color.

With **wrong** sides together, sew Bodies together filling with crinkle material before closing.

Join White with sc to point of Raindrop, ch 7; finish off leaving a long end.

Sew Cloud to one Side Square, filling with crinkle material before closing.

Sew Raindrops to Cloud.

SIDE 4
HEART

First Side (Right side)**:** With Red, ch 3, 11 dc in third ch from hook, slip st in top of beginning ch, sc in next dc, (hdc, dc) in next dc, (dc, tr) in next dc; finish off leaving a long end.

Second Side (Right side)**:** With Red, ch 3, 11 dc in third ch from hook, slip st in top of beginning ch, ch 4 (**counts as one tr**), dc in same st, (hdc, sc) in next dc, sc in next dc, slip st in next 2 dc; finish off.

With **right** sides together, sew tr of Sides together to form point. Skip next 2 dc from point on each Side and sew next dc together.

SQUARE

With Orange, ch 10; join with slip st to form a ring.

Rnd 1 (Right side)**:** ★ Ch 3, 5 dc in ring, sc in top of last dc made and around same dc, sc in ring; repeat from ★ once **more**; do **not** join, place marker to indicate beginning of rnd: 18 sts.

Rnd 2: ★ Sc around next dc, (sc, ch 1, sc) in top of same dc, sc in next 4 dc, (sc, ch 1, sc) in next dc, sc in next 3 sc; repeat from ★ once **more**: 24 sc and 4 ch-1 sps.

Rnd 3: Sc in next 2 sc, ★ (sc, ch 1, sc) in next ch-1 sp, sc in each sc across to next ch-1 sp; repeat from ★ around to marker, remove marker, sc in each sc across to next ch-1 sp; slip st in next ch-1 sp, finish off.

STAR

With Yellow, ch 15; join with slip st to form a ring.

Rnd 1 (Right side)**:** ★ † Ch 4, sc in second ch from hook, hdc in next ch, dc in next ch, skip next 2 chs on ring †, sc in next ch; repeat from ★ 3 times **more**, then repeat from † to † once; join with slip st to joining slip st, finish off.

TRIANGLE

Rnd 1 (Right side)**:** With Dk Green, ch 4, ★ † sc in second ch from hook, hdc in next ch, dc in next ch †, ch 7; repeat from ★ once **more**, then repeat from † to † once, ch 3; join with slip st to free loop of ch at base of first dc: 9 sts and 3 ch-3 sps.

Rnd 2: Ch 1, working in free loops of chs, sc in same st as joining and in next 2 chs, (sc, ch 2, sc) in next ch, sc in next 3 sts, 3 sc in next ch-3 sp, ★ sc in next 3 chs, (sc, ch 2, sc) in next ch, sc in next 3 sts, 3 sc in next ch-3 sp; repeat from ★ once **more**; join with slip st first sc, finish off.

CIRCLE

With Blue, ch 12; join with slip st to form a ring.

Rnd 1 (Right side)**:** Ch 3, dc in same st as joining, 2 dc in next ch and in each ch around; do **not** join, place marker to indicate beginning of rnd: 24 dc.

Rnd 2: (Sc in next 2 dc, 2 sc in next dc) around; slip st in next sc, finish off.

Sew buttons to one Side Square.

BOTTOM
SLIDES

With Red and leaving a long end, ch 30; finish off leaving a long end.

With Orange and leaving a long end, ch 35; finish off leaving a long end.

With Yellow and leaving a long end, ch 25; finish off leaving a long end.

With Dk Green and leaving a long end, ch 15; finish off leaving a long end.

With Blue and leaving a long end, ch 30; finish off leaving a long end.

Sew Slides to last Square.

BEAD (Make 5)

With Variegated, work 6 fdc *(see Foundation Double Crochet, page 44)*; finish off leaving a long end.

Wrap Bead around one Slide. Using long end, sew first and last fdc together.

Repeat for remaining Beads.

BOTTOM

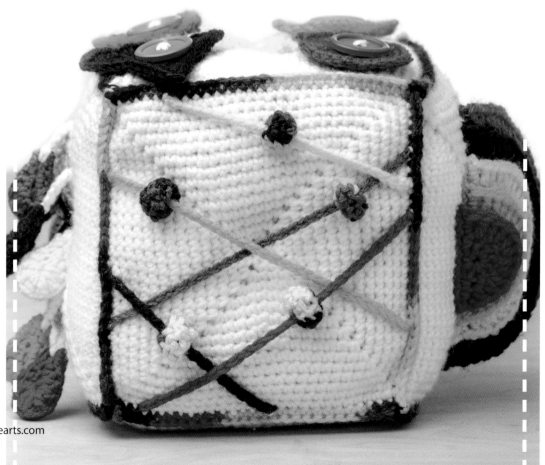

general instructions

ABBREVIATIONS

ch(s)	chain(s)
cm	centimeters
dc	double crochet(s)
fdc	foundation double crochet(s)
fhdc	foundation half double crochet(s)
fsc	foundation single crochet(s)
hdc	half double crochet(s)
mm	millimeters
Rnd(s)	Round(s)
sc	single crochet(s)
sc2tog	single crochet 2 together
sc3tog	single crochet 3 together
sp(s)	space(s)
st(s)	stitch(es)
tr	treble crochet(s)
YO	yarn over

SYMBOLS & TERMS

★ — work instructions following ★ as many **more** times as indicated in addition to the first time.

† to † — work all instructions from first † to second † **as many** times as specified.

( ) or **[ ]** — work enclosed instructions **as many** times as specified by the number immediately following **or** work all enclosed instructions in the stitch or space indicated **or** contains explanatory remarks.

colon (:) — the number(s) given after a colon at the end of a row or round denote(s) the number of stitches and spaces you should have on that row or round.

GAUGE

Exact gauge is **essential** for proper size. Before beginning your project, make the sample swatch given in Basic Square in the yarn and hook specified. After completing the swatch, measure it, counting your stitches and rounds carefully. If your swatch is larger or smaller than specified, **make another, changing hook size to get the correct gauge**. Keep trying until you find the size hook that will give you the specified gauge.

CROCHET TERMINOLOGY		
UNITED STATES		INTERNATIONAL
slip stitch (slip st)	=	single crochet (sc)
single crochet (sc)	=	double crochet (dc)
half double crochet (hdc)	=	half treble crochet (htr)
double crochet (dc)	=	treble crochet (tr)
treble crochet (tr)	=	double treble crochet (dtr)
double treble crochet (dtr)	=	triple treble crochet (ttr)
triple treble crochet (tr tr)	=	quadruple treble crochet (qtr)
skip	=	miss

CROCHET HOOKS																	
U.S.	B-1	C-2	D-3	E-4	F-5	G-6	7	H-8	I-9	J-10	K-10½	L-11	M/N-13	N/P-15	P/Q	Q	S
Metric - mm	2.25	2.75	3.25	3.5	3.75	4	4.5	5	5.5	6	6.5	8	9	10	15	16	19

▮▯▯▯ BEGINNER	Projects for first-time crocheters using basic stitches. Minimal shaping.
▮▮▯▯ EASY	Projects using yarn with basic stitches, repetitive stitch patterns, simple color changes, and simple shaping and finishing.
▮▮▮▯ INTERMEDIATE	Projects using a variety of techniques, such as basic lace patterns or color patterns, mid-level shaping and finishing.
▮▮▮▮ EXPERIENCED	Projects with intricate stitch patterns, techniques and dimension, such as non-repeating patterns, multi-color techniques, fine threads, small hooks, detailed shaping and refined finishing.

MARKERS

Markers are used to help distinguish the beginning of each round being worked. Place a 2" (5 cm) scrap piece of yarn before the first stitch of each round, moving marker after each round is complete.

JOINING WITH SC

When instructed to join with sc, begin with a slip knot on hook. Insert hook in stitch or space indicated, YO and pull up a loop, YO and draw through both loops on hook.

JOINING WITH HDC

When instructed to join with hdc, begin with a slip knot on hook. YO, holding loop on hook, insert hook in stitch or space indicated, YO and pull up a loop (3 loops on hook), YO and draw through all 3 loops on hook.

FOUNDATION SINGLE CROCHET *(abbreviated fsc)*

Ch 2, insert hook in second ch from hook, YO and pull up a loop, YO and draw through one loop on hook (**ch made**), YO and draw through both loops on hook (**first fsc made**), ★ insert hook in ch at base of last fsc made, YO and pull up a loop, YO and draw through one loop on hook (**ch made**), YO and draw through both loops on hook (**fsc made**); repeat from ★ for each additional fsc.

FOUNDATION HALF DOUBLE CROCHET *(abbreviated fhdc)*

Ch 3, YO, insert hook in third ch from hook, YO and pull up a loop, YO and draw through one loop on hook (**ch made**), YO and draw through all 3 loops on hook (**first fhdc made**), ★ YO, insert hook in ch at base of last fhdc made, YO and pull up a loop, YO and draw through one loop on hook (**ch made**), YO and draw through all 3 loops on hook (**fhdc made**); repeat from ★ for each additional fhdc.

FOUNDATION DOUBLE CROCHET *(abbreviated fdc)*

Ch 3, YO, insert hook in third ch from hook, YO and pull up a loop, YO and draw through one loop on hook (**ch made**), (YO and draw through 2 loops on hook) twice (**first fdc made**), ★ YO, insert hook in ch at base of last fdc made, YO and pull up a loop, YO and draw through one loop on hook (**ch made**), (YO and draw through 2 loops on hook) twice (**fdc made**); repeat from ★ for each additional fdc.

Yarn Weight Symbol & Names	LACE 0	SUPER FINE 1	FINE 2	LIGHT 3	MEDIUM 4	BULKY 5	SUPER BULKY 6	JUMBO 7
Type of Yarns in Category	Fingering, size 10 crochet thread	Sock, Fingering, Baby	Sport, Baby	DK, Light Worsted	Worsted, Afghan, Aran	Chunky, Craft, Rug	Super Bulky, Roving	Jumbo, Roving
Crochet Gauge* Ranges in Single Crochet to 4" (10 cm)	32-42 sts**	21-32 sts	16-20 sts	12-17 sts	11-14 sts	8-11 sts	6-9 sts	5 sts and fewer
Advised Hook Size Range	Steel*** 6 to 8, Regular hook B-1	B-1 to E-4	E-4 to 7	7 to I-9	I-9 to K-10½	K-10½ to M/N-13	M/N-13 to Q	Q and larger

*GUIDELINES ONLY: The chart above reflects the most commonly used gauges and hook sizes for specific yarn categories.

** Lace weight yarns are usually crocheted with larger hooks to create lacy openwork patterns. Accordingly, a gauge range is difficult to determine. Always follow the gauge stated in your pattern.

*** Steel crochet hooks are sized differently from regular hooks–the higher the number, the smaller the hook, which is the reverse of regular hook sizing.

ADJUSTABLE LOOP

Wind yarn around two fingers to form a ring *(Fig. 1a)*. Slide yarn off fingers and grasp the strands at the top of the ring *(Fig. 1b)*. Insert hook from **front** to **back** into the ring, pull up a loop, YO and draw through loop on hook to lock ring *(Fig. 1c)* (st made does **not** count as part of beginning ch of first rnd). Working around **both** strands, follow instructions to work sts in the ring, then pull yarn tail to close *(Fig. 1d)*.

Fig. 1a

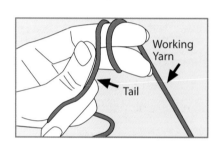

Fig. 1b

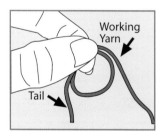

Fig. 1c

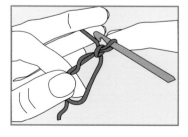

Fig. 1d

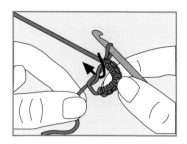

FREE LOOPS

After working in Back or Front Loops Only on a row or round, there will be a ridge of unused loops. These are called the free loops. Later, when instructed to work in the free loops of the same row or round, work in these loops *(Fig. 2a)*.

When instructed to work in free loops of a chain, work in loop indicated by arrow *(Fig. 2b)*.

Fig. 2a

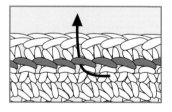

Fig. 2b

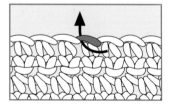

BACK OR FRONT LOOP ONLY

Work only in loop(s) indicated by arrow *(Fig. 3)*.

Fig. 3

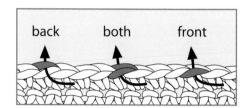

EMBROIDERY STITCHES
STRAIGHT STITCH

Straight stitch is just what the name implies, a single, straight stitch. Come up at 1 and go down at 2 (*Fig. 4*).

Fig. 4

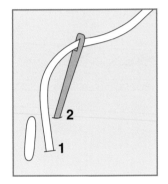

BACKSTITCH

Backstitch is worked from right to left. Come up at 1, go down at 2 and come up at 3 (*Fig. 5*). The second stitch is made by going down at 1 and coming up at 4.

Fig. 5

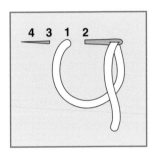

SATIN STITCH

Satin stitch is a series of straight stitches that come out of and go into the same stitches. Come up at 1 and go down at 2 (*Fig. 7*).

Fig. 7

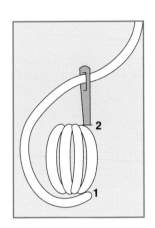

LAZY DAISY STITCH

Make all loops equal in length. Come up at 1 and make a counterclockwise loop with the yarn. Go down at 1 and come up at 2, keeping the yarn below the point of the needle (*Fig. 6*). Secure loop by bringing yarn over loop and down at 3. Repeat for the desired number of petals or leaves.

Fig. 6

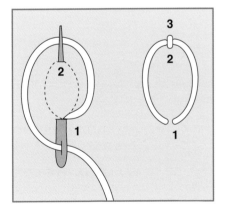

yarn information

Each item in this book was made using Red Heart® Super Saver®, a Medium Weight Yarn. Any brand of Medium Weight Yarn may be used. It is best to refer to the yardage/meters when determining how many balls or skeins to purchase. Remember, to arrive at the finished size, it is the GAUGE/TENSION that is important, not the brand of yarn.

For your convenience, listed below are the specific colors used to create our photography models. Because yarn manufacturers make frequent changes to their product lines, you may sometimes find it necessary to use a substitute yarn or to search for the discontinued product at alternate suppliers (locally or online).

Red - #319 Cherry Red

Burgundy - #376 Burgundy

Blue - #886 Blue

Lt Blue - #381 Lt Blue

Dk Aqua - #506 Pool

Pink - #706 Perfect Pink

Lt Pink - #724 Baby Pink

White - #311 White

Black - #312 Black

Grey - #341 Lt Grey

Dk Grey - #400 Grey Heather

Orange - #254 Pumpkin

Yellow - #324 Bright Yellow

Lt Green - #625 Guava

Green - #368 Paddy Green

Dk Green - #389 Hunter Green

Purple - #776 Dk Orchid

Navy - #387 Soft Navy

Lt Purple - #579 Pale Plum

Gold - #320 Cornmeal

Tan - #334 Buff

Variegated - #950 Mexicana

Production Team: Instructional/Technical Editors - Sarah J. Green, Cathy Hardy, and Lois J. Long; Senior Graphic Artist - Lora Puls; Graphic Artist - Victoria Temple; Photo Stylist - Lori Wenger; and Photographer - Jason Masters.

meet jessica boyer

Jessica Boyer learned to crochet in childhood, taught by her grandmother, but she started crocheting more after she was diagnosed with fibromyalgia in her early twenties. "I like to make amigurumi animals that look semi-realistic and playful," she said. "This is definitely a passion for me, from sketching to crocheting to assembling the pieces."

High school sculptural work and college classes in graphic design have come in handy, she says. "I always work the amigurumi pieces more as I would a soft sculpture. I sketch some quick ideas of what I want the subject to look like, and then I look at as many photos as I possibly can of what I want to make and at every angle possible."

A stay-at-home mom, Jessica loves "cheesy" horror movies, reading, and '90s alternative music. Other arts and crafts that she enjoys are cross stitch, wire jewelry making, and acrylic painting. Look for other Leisure Arts books featuring Jessica's designs at www.leisurearts.com/meet-the-designers/jessica-boyer.html. Visit jessboyercrochet.tumblr.com or find her on Ravelry and Etsy.